D0392349

FOR THE NEW YEAR

WINNER OF THE WALT WHITMAN
AWARD FOR 1984

Sponsored by the Academy of American Poets, the Walt Whitman Award is given annually to the winner of an open competition among American poets who have not yet published their first books of poetry.

JUDGE FOR 1984: MARK STRAND

FOR THE NEW YEAR

Poems by Eric Pankey

ATHENEUM   *New York   1984*

Acknowledgment is gratefully made to the following periodicals in which poems from this book were first published:

The Chariton Review: "Mute Spirits"
Christian Science Monitor: "This Morning"
Crazyhorse: "Reading In Bed"
Intro 13: "To José Del Valle: October, 1981"
The Iowa Review: "Returning In Winter"
Ironwood: "Reasons Of Ice"
The Kansas Quarterly: "Tainter's Farm"
The Kenyon Review: "Encounters"; "On The Way To Singapore"
The Literary Review: "Winter Anniversary"
The Missouri Review: "Tending The Garden"
Poet Lore: "The Gift"; "Vallejo: Paris, 1938"; "The Winter Dinner"
Seneca Review: "A Photograph of My Parents Ice Skating, 1954"
Telescope: "The Politics Of Happiness"
Tendril: "Late August"; "The Guard: 1934"

"Tending The Garden" is influenced and inspired by Pierre Gascar's short story "The Seasons of the Dead."
"After The Japanese" is both imitation and translation of poems by Issa, Buson and Shiki.
"To Olga Knipper" and "On The Way To Singapore" are informed by the letters of Anton Chekhov.

811
Pankey

ISBN 0-689-11507-5 (CLOTH)
    0-689-11506-7 (PAPER)
Published simultaneously in Canada by McClelland and Stewart Ltd.
Composed and printed by Heritage Printers, Inc.,
    Charlotte, North Carolina
Bound by The Delmar Company, Charlotte, North Carolina
Designed by Harry Ford
First Edition

For my mother and in memory of my father

*There had always been a tinge of
melancholy in my conception of human
happiness, and now, confronted by a
happy man, I was overcome by a feeling
of sadness bordering on desperation.*

ANTON CHEKHOV

CONTENTS

REASONS OF ICE

TORNADO WEATHER

TENDING THE GARDEN

REASONS OF ICE

TO OLGA KNIPPER

May 25, 1901 (Yalta)

My little actress,
                    The frail white birch
planted near my favorite seat
was split unluckily by lightning.
When the storm clouds gathered overhead,
the scarlet stars of pimpernel closed.
I watched the two cranes with clipped wings
start their odd waltz through the garden
and around the imported eucalyptus.
Then rain fell: one gray sheet of water
smearing my French window. The garden,
the row of peach and apricot trees,
and the spreading plums with fine red leaves,
looked like the waste of a ruined orchard.
I sat up writing and the rain slowed
until I could make out the details
of the small Japanese trees, the vines.
And the avenue of acacias
in the receding wind, bowed their tips
and drew back up again—restless
and disconsolate in their movements.
The long char on the birch's bleached bark
is ugly—a dark damp glimmering
in the last bit of evening light.
I am not well here without you.
The standard roses are unfortunate
in their beauty, the poplars in their size.
One of the squawking cranes cannot be found.
Someday this long stand of trees will seem
audience enough, and the slight breeze
lifting through the tangle of branches
will endure easily like sadness
or the subtle disappointment felt
after good weather or lovemaking.
The tree may survive. It's hard to say.
Someday. I hope to see you soon.

ON THE WAY TO SINGAPORE

This kind of fear is not new to me.
One night on the inland trip, I woke
to a breeze of dust and mosquitoes.
The moon, liquid and turquoise, reflecting
on the surface of Lake Baikal,
lit the tall grass along the paths
the reindeer sleighs cut into the woods.
I had heard such paths into the forest
when overgrown at the end of spring
might lead to an illegal still
or the encampment of escaped convicts.
I searched for a long while in my bag
for a pocket-knife I swore I had packed
until I was tired again and slept.
Tonight it is easy to imagine
how dark the sea gets beneath the ship
and how carefully a weight might drift
to the soft silt and sediment.
I have to use a handkerchief
all the time, now my cough has begun.
In the evenings I feel feverish.
We have buried two bodies at sea.
When you see a corpse sewn in canvas
hurtled with a slow somersault
into the water behind the stern
and when you remember just how deep
the water grows beneath the ship,
you begin to feel afraid,
and you have the idea that you too
will die and be thrown into the sea.

READING IN BED

Chekhov writes of a man
who loved gooseberries so much
that little else mattered.
His devotion was simple,
complete, yet involved loss,
the way the lack of foliage
in the midst of winter
allows the mind to imagine
the abstraction of a line.
In the story, as now, a sudden rain
taps the window.
As we both sit up reading tonight,
the light from our individual lamps
sets us apart,
the room somehow larger
in the evening's diminishing clarity.
Months from now I will remember
everything I did not say tonight
—how it is possible to love,
how the air at the beginning
of any season smells the same,
the sky different
only in the number of birds
cutting the frail arc of blue . . .
Once I believed that in touching
there was a language that outlives loss.
But now, as you turn out your light,
I am glad I have said nothing
and have instead lived
in another's story for a short while.
I could say I am happy
but I know what I am feeling
is no more permanent
than the narrowness of a road

where it becomes a point on the horizon,
and if I walked down that road
the trees on either side
would grow larger and separate,
detailed, though bare.

A PHOTOGRAPH OF MY PARENTS
ICE SKATING, 1954

The slight mist lifts into the upper branches,
and the branches are a cross-hatching
that suggests shadow, a line.
The line is never exact.
It is what the eye sees
from this perspective, from this attic.
Such a line can be translated
into a thing like sadness,
or more simply, like the fence
the neighbors put up last fall
and now the sloping white
is interrupted by regular posts
and by the iced wire stretching
toward the cluttering of ash and Chinese elm.
If on the other side of the hill,
skaters abandoned the ice
at a particular hour,
how long then before the wind
would smooth the circles of shavings,
the certain arcs catching the last angled light?
Perhaps two lovers remain,
skating until dark,
until whatever music they imagined
became the air
between the blades and the ice,
the unheard creak as ice melts beneath pressure.
They might follow the same lines,
gracefully, without thought
until the light fails finally.
And as they walk back to the house,
the ice behind them
might give way to the darkness
like a skylight beneath the weight of snow.
These lines remind me how as a child
I would trace my name
again and again
until I was sure it was my own,

until it was something separate and believable.
My father would call me in then from the dark.
The stars loitering
against the smeared black
seemed as close as the flecks of light
on the icy street below my window.
Once in Vermont, from the high balcony
of a hotel called the Winter Chateau,
I would look down
at the few pedestrians
stumbling along the road into town.
I would spit
and lose my spit in the whiteness below.
I was five. *Chateau*—
I thought I was in another country.
All day thin fog
lifted off the indoor swimming pool.
If I went back there would be no such hotel,
no couples walking beneath the sagging branches,
nor the odd breathing of my parents
asleep in the next bed;
as tonight, the couple I see walking
toward the house is not in love
and the skates slung over their shoulders
are for this moment only awkward weights
they carry to keep their balance
along the rutted path.
As they enter the house,
they will not hear me
rummaging above them in this attic
and they will talk quietly
as if not to wake someone.

TO JOSE DEL VALLE, OCTOBER, 1981

I walked home last night
through the clear dark
and felt cool air within my lungs—
the air just before the first frost.
I thought of how I had sat
in the corner booth at the Three Cheers Lounge
one night in early winter
and looking up at that moment
when conversation seemed to cease naturally,
I watched snow begin on Eighth Street.
The snow fell
as if the story you were telling
called for such an element.
It hardly looked like snow—
more like settling ash
or the rain at night
when it slows suddenly before it stops.
The snow is not what I remember most,
but the realization that a change in weather
does change our lives,
at least for a moment.
I remember talking about the end
of Joyce's *The Dead*—
how you said the snow will always fall,
that Gabriel will never turn away from the window,
from that still scene
growing whiter than anything
we might call pure. What I held inside
that night, I cannot remember—
it was not like snow
filling the fine cracks in the pavement,
but more like a promise we make
we know we will never keep.
Maybe the promise sustains us. I don't know.
I left that night
and walked home along Broadway,

waiting at times beneath awnings
for the wind to die.
In the morning there was no snow,
just grass turning to the dull black of mud.
It will be winter soon.
I stare out my window often,
but the change is so subtle
I get bored.
Ending here is easy—*good-bye*—
because endings are always flawed.
You can put down this letter
the way I put a book down—
the lives in the story
stopped, forgotten perhaps,
until something takes me back,
reminds me I am just like them,
but not them.
It was raining in the story.
It's raining here. Coincidence.

OLD SAYBROOK

The ray must have been looking for something
swimming those few yards inland up the marsh creek
—its wing's white flesh trapped in ice,
its eyes pecked out by gulls.
I broke the ice with the toe of my boot
and the ray turned belly-up.
It did not wash out to sea, or sink.
It bobbed where the two waters met.
The creek separated me
from a tangle of tide-line vegetation,
from the waves turning into residual foam.
And the sun burned,
the one thing for that moment not blue or white.

What I could taste and smell in the air
was salt and the rot of that ray.
The ice had not preserved it.
I could have crossed to the shore
on a plank children used
all summer to their fort among the brambles.
Sun caught on the rose hips,
on the small pool's iced edge
where glacial stones had washed out.
Marsh grass rustled yellow, white.
I knew by now the kitchen
would be warm, filled with light,
and you would be waking.

THIS MORNING

Hoarfrost flowers on the stubble,
and catches first light as it glints
off the snow-filled furrows.

                       This white
beneath the cloud-shadow's slow blue
is a privacy turning outward, unfolding—
like the shape of water overflowing
a leaf-clogged gutter—how it freezes
in the moment of its fall.

                     This morning.
This quiet as the streetlight clicks off,
and the gray horse, its mane hatched in ice slivers,
tears at the bent, shagged stalks.

WINTER ANNIVERSARY

Again this year the moonlight
creates a road of ice-filled ruts.
Tonight, the branches hold back
beneath a tree-load of birds
that shudder all at once, and lift.
In the field, the horse's mane
is distinct, shaggy with hoarfrost;
its slow breath, faint and earthly,
holds the light still as we walk.
Words we were speaking
have become a fine quiet steam.
Tonight, the space between us
grows dense with its own gravity.
The season has returned as we have
—still indifferent, still faithful.

The purple-leaved plum blooms
in March, as it should. And this snow,
in its time, falls around us as well.
How can we not smile at the oddity—
blossoms covered with thin ice shells.
Early flowers? A late snow?
We know as we give in to sleep
a year will have passed
as easily as a gray horse
disappearing beyond a stand of maples,
light from the frozen river.
In the morning the bark is black
with melt and the sun is out.
We know this before it happens—
there is, after all, only ice,
the water dripping beneath it, then freezing,
still months before a real thaw.

RETURNING IN WINTER

after Czeslaw Milosz

Think what you will about this place where we have come—
the light settled on gray silt, the creekbed choked with leaves,
a fine mud, the clay of the bank tumbling in.

I cannot remember myself here before, now that it is winter
and the snow begins to fall.

The paths are empty, smooth where no one has walked. Soon,
eroded gullies will be drifted full of snow.

I could believe that without wind the tall dried grass would
continue to lean away.

I could believe that in summer vines tangle around the unkept
hedges, the red thorns and ripened berries lining the thin
green limbs.

I could believe that, yes, I lived here once with you, instructed
by nothing I would know enough to remember. I pull my coat
around me and listen. There is the cold, the ice creaking in the
trees. The clear sound of the world beyond forgiveness.

We were so wise then. We believed cruelty was weather, and
could change.

REASONS OF ICE

The house sits up ahead on the hill
—the roof white, weighted with a whole month's fall.
It's quiet here. There's no sound
from the schoolyard or from the snow-owl
whose wing shadow looks like a blue blade
against the birch. Even as the owl
falls into flight, there's only my breathing.
Today, old snow grays in the ditchbank.
The spruces shag in hoods of frost.
And the owl, in its one beauty,
is a thing I cannot touch.
I would like to hold this still world,
if the world were a thing to be held.
But it's here beneath me, solid,
with the same punctual cold.

I was surprised when I walked out this morning
by the suddenness of light, silver
on the mountain laurel's green—a color out of place
above the snow's sooty tatterings.
I must have been looking for something
—something that would survive this ice,
its sheathing. All I am left with now
is detail: the birch mottled with lichen,
the rust and yellow-white of ground cover,
the Christmas fern's thin shuddering
beneath the sag of hemlock.
It seems, now, there is nothing beautiful
about the owl as it settles
upon an oak's stiff limb,
nothing beautiful about its patience,

its eyes, in shade, darker than mud,
its large fist of a head cowlicked.

AFTER THE JAPANESE

A stand of winter trees

White dew frozen on the prickle of briar
The stubbled fields without snow
can lose nothing else

Only the evergreens
grow dark above the icy soil

Again, all night, snow
and deep in the valley
a young pine is buried

Along this pond's edge
wild ducks, the thin ice forming

Late winter drizzle
A small boat with a boy on board
crosses the river

Floating past it among the ice,
a dead dog's carcass
someone has thrown in

Behind the clouds dropping
winter's last snow, the moon
does not look like *moon*

In the soon-to-thaw fields
tufts of grass on the red earth,
the spotted shapes of unconcerned horses,
daffodil leaves bent beneath white.

TAINTER'S FARM

Everything in the landscape
shares enough to be contradictory.

The ice on the pond thaws
from the edge inward,

and fails to reflect the single cloud
or ragged border of hedgerow.

Beneath the ice, the thin air
holds the residue of another season—

the stale evening air of a day
when the flat gray land

settled into itself,
as the blue shadow and late fog

became the same shade of terrain.
For a moment, the underbrush

caught bits of light,
and whatever was passing

above the branches
could no longer be translated

into the detail of wings
or an escape into a climate

I would not share.
At the end of winter

it is easy to talk in the past tense,
as though each wind adds to the erasures,

to the white sky holding,
by now, nothing.

FALSE SPRING

I look into a stubbled field,
obvious in its emptiness after an early thaw,
and I am certain that the dew
catches the same light
that shimmered dry frost in early winter.
Such certainty comes down to desire—
desire for that moment,
for the bit of fragile light offering nothing
but its own preciousness—
simple reflected sunlight
lifting, as it does, over a field.
Once, I believed noticing it
at that precise moment
changed everything,
and after that moment, I'd be beyond desire.
But this morning,
such logic is only that—logic.
Nothing is easy.
The light from this sodden field
is far from blinding.
It settles on the little flesh-colored mushrooms,
on the black shiny mold
blooming on damp leaf-muck.
In shade, strips of snow
remain unthawed
after the flat lands have become marshes
and the creeks black with rain and runoff.
One yellow jacket,
coaxed by a week of warm weather,
hovers awkwardly above scraps of corn stalks.
It seems as tired as I am,
and confused.
If it longs for anything,
it is not for the beads of moisture
clinging to its legs' black fur,

and not for a flowerless field
turning to rot.
I am sure, now, it is tired.
It longs for none of the trouble
the season has created for it.
It stalls, then lifts
in its bright spasm of flight.
It knows it's been fooled.

FOR THE NEW YEAR

for Jennifer

White walls kept white, rubbed with chalk

and limewater. The sun, now,
released from behind storm clouds

is opening somehow—white
upon the winter water.

The whole house skirted with snow.

Snow fills the bamboo basket.
One straw-colored sparrow flits.

A dusk-brown deer, flecked with white,
nudges the round tufts of moss.

The yellow of pine needles.
Yes, these are generous days.

The duck marinates in dry
red wine. Stuffed with potatoes,

one recipe says, or fresh
cranberries and wild rice,

it is a holiday meal.
Although the flesh is dark

and sometimes slightly bitter.

Once, on a stalled bus, in March,
I woke to a child's soft voice

explaining, "No, Mom,—you're wrong.
You shouldn't draw it like that!

A heart looks more like a fist."

Rose hips seen from iced windows.

The taste of mollusk. Mushrooms
cooked in garlic and butter.

The still cold brought in on coats.
Nothing's sad about darkness.

The clear dark of cabernet.

This is what I wanted most:

the snow revealing itself,
the slow kind laughter of friends,

a dust of frost, a morning's
tender dull blue arriving.

This light after the body's
pleasure. Always this light.

TORNADO WEATHER

AMONG WEEDS, WILD FLOWERS

The warm breeze
before it reaches me
stirs the wild licorice,
the stinging nettle,
and purple phlox spilling dew.
Poised in damp shadow,
the bent head
of a jack-in-the-pulpit—
like natural humility
you suggested once to me.
And at my feet now,
another example, it seems—
Solomon's seal,
a long bow of green stem
beneath the white
weight of blossoms.
There is grief
in beauty—it grows wild
in woods like these.
The earth holds undergrowth
for its own beauty
by something as simple
as gravity—
whether it be pineapple grass,
poison ivy, or dandelion
coloring the clay gray soil.
Or weeds we have not learned
but whose roots might brew
a curative tea
and offer a flower
that blooms only at night
—a color the dark
beneath shadow cannot hide,
as now, on the blackbird's
smooth wings, red flashes
within the deep green leaves.

THE GIFT

No one is waiting. No one watches
the mist and few stars as they gather.
Somehow you are the only one to see
the rain as it starts.

You have learned to love the late hour,
the detail of stillness
—everything the color of rain in darkness.

In an hour, the pale moon will mean nothing
more than morning and an equally blank sky.
It offers you nothing. I give you this.

Something simple, ordinary.
Something you might learn to fear.

LATE AUGUST

While you are packing,
I go upstairs to write.
All the house's left-over heat
follows me up, it seems.
I sit by an open window
and sweat.
Nothing comes.
You have on the same album
you've played all summer.

Saxophones. A beat up record—
swing and jazz.
Gerry Mulligan, Stan Getz
and some other great I should know.
I try not to listen.
For a minute, I watch a mud-dauber
build its nest in a shutter slat.
A sliver of light
follows its body's thin curve,

a body balanced carefully
between flicks of wings
doing business with the air.
It starts to rain.
Lines of drops
gather on the shutter's edge,
each weighted with a fine mud.
The wasp continues
until I lose its shape

in the splatterings of dirt
on the driveway and the quick
irregular lines of water
blurring the window.
As always, I am watching.

As always, the record skips
on a low note, skips
three or four times
before you get to it.

I am pleased
for the first time
by the variation,
by the interruption,
and can't imagine the song
any other way.
I can hear the bath water
running as I watch
the screen smear with rain.

There is a breeze,
a thick slow wind still full of heat,
but it is motion, a relief.

FIRES

This morning we found,
in steam that was dew
earlier on undergrowth,
Solomon's seal, blossoms withered,
the thin whip of stem
bent with fruit.
Not cool in the moist heat,
in shadow,
the blue flesh, almost black,

was drawn tight and shiny.
The motes of seeds suspended
in dark, certainly bitter juice.
Tiny blue berries
we dared not taste
and of which the field guide says little,
fruit the mockingbird,
perched above in the low raspberries,
ignored. Tonight,

our bodies are heavy with heat,
the season's poison.
Above the slow tide of humidity,
the useless moon.
What it cannot hold
it gives back as light,
as we give back salt,
what has become too much
to carry.

We wait for a breeze
that might cool us,
that might cover our damp skin.
When you sleep,
I sit up and listen
to the neighbors argue.

This would be the hour for a walk.
If I were not so tired
I could leave you

here. The heat will hang
high in the maples
until morning.
In the thicket, berries
are indistinguishable
from other specklings of light and dark.
At this hour, above the neighbor's yard,
fireflies, slow, weighted with light,
feed on mosquitoes—

the dull glow dissolving,
reappearing. Small miracles
firing the air.

STORMS

After a storm unbraided itself,
our neighbors burned debris—
torn branches, jagged planks,
siding pulled clean
from a house three blocks away,
and a broken trellis
woven tight with a rose's
thin green wood.
It was the day you decided
to leave. Above the fire,
as the rain started again,
swirls of steam
knotted with black smoke
and hung twisting over the fire.
I can't remember
what you said that day.
I remember I let go
of your hand, and a breeze
working its way around the flames
cooled against my palm.
Now, whatever sadness
I felt is mixed with pleasure,
memory. Earlier that summer
the water of the strip pits
held our bodies up.
Dark water red with clay.
Clouds—the afternoon
exchanging light and dark
as the wind flattened on the water.
The maples along the hillside,
the white of leaves upturned,
shuddered as light broke.
Then shadow. We'd take turns
seeing who could touch bottom.
You'd disappear with a splash,

the water would smooth
and I'd be alone.
I'd listen to cars,
a radio's noise lingering
in the billow of dust, or
I'd watch a bat repeat
its level circle above the water and pit-edge.
Once, when you'd been down
for I don't know how long,
I pushed myself under, feet-first,
but couldn't, in my panic, make it
to the bottom. When I broke
the surface, you were laughing.
And so I laughed. I could taste
the copperous water, heavy air.
Above the limestone bluffs,
black clouds stacked up,
a squall line. No wind.
Only our strokes and the first drops
disturbed the water.

ENCOUNTERS

1.
He began to climb the slender tree,
his weight familiar beneath him as he pulled.
Where the waxy leaves grew thin, he could look down
over the whole of California, Missouri
and into where the birches stopped around a small pool
fed by a local creek, and in the pool, a woman
bathing, he supposed, her back to him
as he watched her slow movements,
how her hands vanished beneath the surface,
the water clinging to her waist, a loose garment.
When he called to her, she turned
and he was surprised when she did not speak
or try to hide her body from him, a boy.
And he watched as she walked into the center,
silently, a white figure descending into blue.

2.
Once, during the Occupation, he left the bars
early, before the curfew and followed
footpaths into the woods above Kyōto.
He watched as a storm approached
and the coppery tops of trees grew green-black
dark as water when the fishing boats return.
Each lightning flash made mist glow around him
like mist in the landscapes of an illustrated volume.
He felt at home beneath the trees' shadow
as the bluebells turned gray along the path
and as the slight slope of the single mountain disappeared in
    fog.
And then rain. Ending quickly with a cool breeze,
the odd scent of torn spruce, the leafmold black, shining.
Below, two farmers crossed a field toward home,
their conversation unheard from where he stood.

One listened intently; the other talked, gestured,
as if it were a story they had heard many times
and yet loved to tell again. As they talked,
faint steam lifted from the eroded furrows,
almost unnoticeable against the settling evening.

ELEGY

Sure, the earth gives back what it chooses.
The small body of dust it once held.
The rainclouds huddled above the house.
A grief we articulate as love,
As if it were love. Something I'd asked for.

It does not matter that the evening
Arrives as always. Faithful, measured.
It's what I've come to expect. This waiting.
The curiosity of weather.
The rain that comes. The rain you're made of.

Now, there is little I can give you.
The wind that passes through the window,
The windchime's racket, the cool freshness.
It's all a sort of lovemaking. Pain
I can enjoy in its precision,

That takes the shape of everything I own.

A WALK WITH MY FATHER

A columbine's clear violet after noon rain.

The ditch of a creek we'd followed here,
muddy water stippled with shadow. It is 1966.
On the bank, a carp, or what was left of one,

covered with a glow of flies. Green, gold,
a momentary body of light
lifted as he turned the fish over with a stick.

The exposed flesh was flat, white,
raw as wound. Unearthly.
Or too much of the earth:

the dull texture of clay, the dust white of lime.

To satisfy me, he pushed it over the grassy bank.
The heat was visible on the rank air,
rising against a drift of daisies.

I followed the fish downstream until it caught on rocks
—pale jutted limestone, and the slow water
worked its gill. Opening, open, as if that would help.

SMOKE

My brother and I cut a tunnel
into a border of flowerless
rose bushes that separated
one square rutted field from another.

At dusk, in the hollow we had cut,
the thorn branches tangled above us
—a clumsy loosening weave
of the jay's nest tumbled by wind.

Last light fell in pale scribblings
upon our hands and faces as we worked.
And we worked hard. The place was our own.
My brother hid his trinkets

in a hole we'd dug in the red clay floor:
the skull of a robin rubbed smooth by rain,
matches, steel pennies from 1943,
and fossils—*sea grass* he told me

from when the whole plain was covered
with ocean. He knew about such things.
Once, we risked a fire of twigs and dried leaves.
As it burned, I added strands of green vine

and damp greasy smoke filled the hedge.
At least a hundred grand-daddy-long-legs
fell into our hair, and around us,
and those that fell into the fire

gave off a sickening smell of sulfur.
We were sure it was some sort of magic.
The fire moved up the arc of limbs.
The rain of spiders would not stop.

By then, our father was calling us in, but
we could not see the porch light, or
his figure black against the screen-door.
We knew we were in for it now.

Smoke spread through the tunnel. The dark
was close enough to fill the cracks.

TORNADO WEATHER

This evening in the settling dark,
in what my father called tornado weather,
I watch the heat lift its shimmering weight
above the snapdragons and low sumac
into what light remains inside the maples.

Those long nights while I was up,
sick, heavy with heat and dreams,
I was sure it was my father's broad palm
pressed against my forehead
that held the fever in.

I am no better without him.
If the dark brings with it relief, a chill,
it is a trick—weather storing up its storm.
June bugs rattle the screen, annoying as ever,
like the song he murmured that would not let me sleep.

GHOST OF A CHANCE

It is all here—thistle, ground cherry,
The season's rot: perfect betrayal.

A season dull with weeds and rain.
And on the clear nights, the usual stars.

You are what I do not have tonight.
The calm of sleep, a ghost of a chance.

You are the body pain takes, or takes back.
I am tired of the heat, the old worn

Knot this blood traces through my body.
I forgot how heavy you could be.

TENDING THE GARDEN

MUTE SPIRITS

Horatio at Elsinore

There were other ghosts.
Your cousin, a boy your own age
who walked slowly to the center of a pond on a dare.
A thin crust of ice, almost yellow like old paper
in the noon of an early winter,
covered the water—the circular pond
where you and the young prince
caught spiny-finned perch in the summer months.

Two oval curled leaves clung to the iced tips
of a high beech branch tilting over the pond.
The ice cracked, not suddenly
but like the crust of hard bread as it bakes.
And the boy did not move—
like the stems of the two dried leaves
his feet were trapped in ice.

Without struggling, he fell into the still white water
and drowned.

When he entered your room those nights,
his hair still wet, his clothes dripping
the way trees drip in an intermittent rain,
you could hear footsteps
and were surprised by their solid sound
—a ghost of flesh!
Wet and somewhat blue against the moon's light.

He said nothing.
Entered, then left, like a servant
who forgets his particular errand
and keeps moving from room to room, seemingly busy.

You thought his lungs must be ice,
heavy as glass, which kept him from becoming air.
*   *   *

Tonight you tell the prince an old dream—
It is the night poor Yorick died.
All night you hear him coughing,
sounding at times like laughter,
the aimless laughter of a lunatic.
You have imagined his lungs
to be the wings of a giant red butterfly
floating outside in the soft rain.
Each drop burns a perfect hole
in the wing's thin taut flesh . . . .

Then, in the dawn mist above the peat bog,
a long mooing as a newborn calf tumbles
onto the damp white clover in the dark.

In the morning there are no ghosts,
only the snow-like clover, butterflies,
the unstabled stumblings of the pied calf
and Hamlet, awkward in his young body,
crying, hugging his father,
six years to the day before the king's murder,
while the king, standing in a long robe
like the cloak of a spirit in a street play,
knows no words to explain this first death to his son.

THE WINTER DINNER

When the hunter returned
bringing in with him on the damp leather of his boots
the musty air of a winter dusk,
he found no supper waiting,

and he stood in the doorway, motionless,
while outside wild geese trailed one another,
gray against the graying sky,

and not far from the pond
the skaters abandoned an hour earlier,
in a room above the tavern,
his daughter removed her apron
as if part of a dance, and then her blouse,

the brown tips of her breasts as tight as fists,
while her young man laughed and drank,
tilted his chair back at a dangerous angle.

Her father stepped outside for a moment
to a snow beginning to fall,
and then back inside to the last coals of the fire,

and on the small rosewood table he found only
sliced oranges on a pale blue plate
and painted on an empty frail ceramic vase,
violets and wild strawberries.

VALLEJO: PARIS, 1938

1.

In the gray-green of a photograph
it is hard to tell if you have fallen asleep
or if, leaning against a boulder
white with lichen, green with moss,
you are in prayer.

Your eyes are shadow,
the same darkness of your long black coat.
If you put on the felt hat
you hold in your hand
your thin face would fade
into the haze of trees
that try, but cannot halo your short uneven hair.

All this darkness has weight
and you have measured it
and carried it these years.

2.

You said you would die in Paris on a Thursday—
but it was a Friday—Good Friday—
when any angry man could die
in his loneliness on an unfamiliar road
or in a rented room he could not afford.

There was a small rain, sudden,
unnoticed by the shopkeepers
and then the clouds separated
like witnesses from a streetcorner.

Already in the south, the Fascists
cut their way to the Mediterranean.
A few late sleepers pressed onto the avenue.
And from a fever you cried,
Voy a España . . . .

ST. JEROME

1.

Outlined in the light of burning brush
are the three boys who started the fire.
Their movements are odd and animated,
their faces occasionally lit from below.
Bits of white ash lift, glowing red
in the dry air of late September.
The boys are drunk and one is singing.
No one else is on the street tonight.
Long shadows move up and down the buildings,
wave-like until it seems I too am drunk.
The warm air within my chest, for once,
possesses a precise, unsettling heaviness.
My eyes are bad. I have to squint to see.
Since the boys are but shadow before a fire,
I expect their ghost-weight to lift
above the white branches like smoke.

2.

When I was young I'd prowl the catacombs
deciphering inscriptions,
identifying martyrs and confessors.
Once in my clumsiness, I dropped a lamp.
Oil splashed onto my robe
and onto yellowed paper-like cloth,
the tattered habit of a skeleton.
I remember the thick scent of burning hair or skin
which was, thank God, not my own.
Somehow the martyr's flesh and his wrap
had in the dampness become the same gray gauze.
And now, smoldering, gave off a thick, black smoke.
The frayed ends of my robe were on fire
and I fell to the floor and rolled in a puddle . . . .
A thin ceiling of fog hung in the tunnel.

The place had the smell of the earth
or a thing the body never knows itself to be.

3.
The translucent shell of a cicada
clings to a pine and shudders in the breeze.
If I listened close enough perhaps I'd hear
the wind whistle across the tear in the shell
through which the insect entered again into its life.
This morning the wind found its way
through my window and I woke from a dream:
With my left hand I hold a lamb
by the apricot wool above its eyes,
and with my right pull a knife across its throat.
Where blood should have been there was nothing—
a knife's perfect narrowness disappearing
into flesh easily, like a hand through water.
First light flares, now, in the pine's low limbs.
Sleep is no good when it is murderous.

TO ABEL

I give it up—the earth, what it held for me.
I give it to you, brother, like a caress.
You can have the hills, the dull grazing flock,
the night fire on the eroded embankment.

You can own it all for this one moment.
You can trust me like weather, like shadow,
like the creek striped with reflections of cattails.
You can always trust the familiar.

Take this handful of grain I offer you.
Take this long last look which is a blessing.
Take the air within your lungs for granted.
Take this, brother, which is all I can give you.

Take this blow with forgiveness, as a gift.

THE GUARD: 1934

1.
Sometimes I wake up at night
and don't know where I am.
There's the train beneath me, a scent of dogwood . . . .
Waking is answer enough.
On the boxcar's side, a few damp leaves
are pasted, and the moonlight
shining through them and through the space
between slats is the thin brown-orange
of tea my mother used to make.
Every inch of the boxcar
is a changing shade of brown—
a color that won't stand still.
And always the smell of chickenshit.
Chickenshit. I hate that word.
That's what my brother called me
when I wouldn't join him
and the neighbor boys in the pranks they'd pull.
One time and for no good reason
they put a .22 up the ass
of a mean brindle sow.
My brother said her tits were uglier
than a fat woman's he had seen
at a freak show. But he lied.
He'd never been to one,
never even seen a woman's tits.
And how can something be ugly
when you see it your whole life?
There was no telling what killed the pig
—no wound. Just a crust of brown blood
along the line of the mouth,
blood matting the few jowl hairs.
Its thick flesh was a white, turning gray,
like talc dusted onto sweaty skin
when the only weather there is is humid.

It was noon by the time
the farmer found the sow.
I imagined by then
a fistful of flies covered
its eyes like so many seeds
in the middle of a sunflower.
It seemed like a waste. What's the point?—
I asked my brother. Don't you see, he laughed,
It don't mean a thing, not a thing.

2.
I get to where I can forget
the noise of the chickens, the train's clanking.
This is my fifth trip.
Sometimes when we pass a field
where someone is burning off hawkweed
or where, above the undergrowth
cluttering a creekbank,
peppermint grows,
I can almost ignore the stench.
But then a warm breeze passes through,
and you would think that would help . . . .
As we move on, the wind forces
shit-stink into my nose.
                          At times,
the motion of the train
makes me sick to my stomach.
I slide the door open
but that only makes things worse—
the sun's glare racing on the water
which has gathered in the ditch,
the haze of heat lifting off that water,
the spiderwebs in the maples.
It all moves by too quickly,
all one blurred line like a wall.
The best bet is to focus
on something in the distance.
It doesn't matter what—a hawk,
a shack built up on a rise.

Once I watched a farmer
take a switch to his boy;
I mean, I thought it was his boy.
The scene, at such a distance,
was still, framed by solitary trees.
My stomach seemed to settle.
I don't know how many times
he hit the kid or why.
I just watched until the train darkened
into the length of a tunnel
and I felt better. I felt okay.

3.

I went into town for a half-hour—
Joplin, Missouri. The train stopped
to take on water. I needed a drink.
Although Joplin's just a bunch of Baptists,
you can buy a pint of bourbon
and even a woman if you want.
As I was leaving town, the rain started.
When you have a mile to go
you might as well walk—
no need to run like girls in the rain
from church to their daddy's new auto.
You can only get so wet.
I wasn't supposed to leave the train.

In the boxcar I call my office,
I was drying myself off with an old feedsack.
I heard boards snapping and the chickens
stirring in crates at the car's end.
I had not lit the lantern yet—
I could see all right.
By then the shotgun was loaded
and the coolness of the butt
surprised me when I pulled it
into the shallow of my shoulder.
It felt good against my still damp skin.
I knew what I could do with it.

All I could see was an arm,
striped with railroad yard lights
that angled in through the slats.
It seemed whiter than it should be—
like that of a man who wore
long sleeves even late into July,
or a healed arm fresh out of a cast.
It was kind of frightening,
this arm without a body.
Its hand kept groping at chickens
until it caught one by the claw.
It was a left arm.
I had to imagine the man's face and body
pressed against the boxcar's side—
the man on his tiptoes as he reached in,
the boards rough against his cheek.
I aimed a little to the right.
I didn't care about the chickens anymore.

4.
After this evening's rain,
there's rust settled like brown soot
in the nicks and scratches.
But I take care of this gun—
don't get me wrong.

I can see just fine
through the splintered hole.

My brother told me something once
about the blood inside the body,
how it is blue. Something to do with air.
Nothing blue about this blood—
not even beneath the moon's light
which is almost blue in the puddles
along the tracks and on the tips of pines.

It's what you expect it to be.
Not pretty. Not bad enough to make you sick.

I killed a man with this shotgun.
It was easy. Easier than keeping rust
off the barrel's blue metal.
Almost too easy.
                      As we move beyond a hedgerow,
it's as though a flash of sunlight
fills the car. It's just lightning against the dark.
Although there is coal smoke in the air
and a cool breath of snow, out of season,
as we pass the Joplin Ice Plant,
all I can smell is gunpowder.
I like that smell. The taste of the air.

THE POLITICS OF HAPPINESS

So I said— this is what I am,
as though that would change things,
as though the good morning
offered itself as another chance.
I thought I'd given up on myself,
on memory . . . .
But one thing I remembered
was the first light's unexpected gift
and the dust gathered gracefully
on the window sill's whiteness.
Another thing: the random
but necessary indignities we call pain.
So today
I am resigned to happiness.
The daylight cares little about my joy
if it cares at all.
And it cannot—
the way the new year
can be nothing more than a measurement
of the wind's magnitude
in the sycamore's upper branches,
a measurement of kind, yet waning nostalgia.
I admit to guilt, to a pleasant pride
I wear like an old sweater.
And often at my back
there is a wind
like the hands of a guardian angel
I can almost stop believing in.
I cannot deny that.
So I am a happy man.
I collect sorrows like irregular pieces of string
and if they were string,
I'd tie them in square knots
for no particular reason.
I say to myself, with advice,

as I would to a friend—Look at the moon;
why, it's so pale against the morning's
ivory sky!
It must believe itself precious
to hang on so tirelessly.
This happiness is a curse,
although to love it
is to call it something else.

THE HORSE

The horse my mother sits on is pocked
with dry red clay from the gully.
And as always, the horse will fall

when the five o'clock whistle blows,
when the light glints off the rusted roof
and workers leave the cannery.

Today she is fifteen years old.
She is cool in her cotton dress.
The horse breathes beneath her slowly.

The worn stirrups dangle empty.
Brown chestnut oaks creak in the wind.
Above hills rutted with erosion

a horse buckles beneath its weight.
It lands with a thud against rock.
The hull of its body. The air,

hot and damp within its shape, forced out.

———————————

I have chased it here to this pond,
or what was once a pond, but now,
in the dry season is a marsh.

The one shot muffled to a clap
cracks the horse's hard-boned forehead.
It sinks into the gray green ooze,

the mud grows up its side like mange.
The blood like oil on the water.
At dusk, only its head remains

above the surface, black, outlined
with faint scribblings of moonlight.
It's my duty to watch the horse

until its eyes are covered and
the last bit of air escapes its lungs,
until it's irretrievable,

until someone comes to relieve me.

———————————

In a borrowed car's torn back seat,
mother's brother sits with a gun
pressed against the roof of his mouth.

Beyond the hills of white maple
evening is rehearsing itself.
And with a click night replaces

the farm machinery, the horse
rotting in the renderer's truck,
the lovers parked along the road.

With a click the rear window burns
like a ditch full of wild flowers,
a deep blue red against darkness.

My mother waits on the roadside,
lit up white by the two headlights.
Sweat makes the soiled dress cling to her.

The only thing she can do is wait.

TENDING THE GARDEN

A prisoner-of-war graveyard outside the
disciplinary camp of Brodno in Volynia

1.
The clod of earth in his shovel
was a familiar weight
he had lifted and set aside all day.
by noon, his hands were a dull orange of rust.
If in the wood's damp shadow
white smoke lifted through the branches,
he did not see it, nor did he hear
the whistle yet, releasing steam—its sound
trailing behind the train, the train moving
toward him and the other prisoners
—some digging graves, some planting flowers.
All he knew of death was its weight
as he lowered the bodies by worn ropes
to the moist soil dark with leafmold.
He knew each day there would be new dead.
It did not matter. It was a matter of waiting:
typhus, pneumonia, a frail body limp
in the barbed fence.

He leaned on his shovel and listened
to the train's slow jolting
as it emerged from the trees.
He knew he could dig all day
and it would be useless—only a hole, not a tunnel . . . .
At a certain depth he would climb out
and begin again. There was no other end.
It was best to have a few dug in advance.
Canvas could be stretched over to keep the rain out
and boards placed against the walls
to keep the sides from tumbling in.
As the sun came out from the thick clouds,
a raw gleam of light fell
on the boxcars, then alternate slants of shadow.
He knew what freight the train carried—
white faces framed by narrow slats.

2.

I was luckier than most, luckier
because I don't remember the pain
if there was pain—only the oddity
of tending a graveyard and flowerbeds;
how we convinced the Germans to give us
the materials to build a white fence—
a small luxury for our unnamed dead
and for ourselves. It was our livelihood
to find enough work to last the whole day
before we would have to go back to camp,
back to the dirty barracks where we slept.
The other prisoners were envious
of our duty. It was, at times, hard work,
but the work, it seems, promoted our health.
I was determined to stay well, to last
through the coming winter and not end up
face up in a grave my own hands had dug.

Ernst, the eldest guard, chose to befriend me
and offered me hot tea and cigarettes.
He spoke French as poorly as I spoke German.
He said he was Catholic and we shared that
at least. And though I was not Catholic,
his believing it was a thing to share.
He did not understand the war, but joined
because there was little work, and his wife
had left him earlier that year. He thought
she had joined a circus. One had passed through
town the same week she decided to leave.
It was a story he liked to believe.

I thought I loved a woman then. A girl.
I met her only once. She walked the road
below the graveyard before noon, two pails
of water in her hands, a white armlet
on her sleeve. I believe her name was Sarah.
She must be dead by now. She might have died
shortly after the last day I saw her.
They were collecting Jews near Brodno then.

60

On her armlet was the Star of David.
I might have kissed her that day by the road
but I did not. Ernst wouldn't have cared.
But now, nothing as obvious as a kiss
could reinvent that girl or change anything.

3.
That night he woke on the wooden bunk
and his feet were cold, his neck stiff.
They were given no straw to sleep on
for fear of propagating lice.
Above him, a Russian prisoner laughed in his sleep.
At times the laughter caught in his throat
and it sounded like a man choking.
He tried not to look too closely at the ill.

That night he dreamed winter had come and passed.
The rain and thaw washed away the unpaved streets
and duckboards were thrown down
to let the soldiers pass.
A line of villagers stood motionless,
the muddy water around their ankles,
their armlets gray in rain.
The train was delayed . . . .

That night he woke on the wooden bunk
and realized if despair can be held,
it has the weight of a tuft of earth
and is bitter held close to the face.
It is what might cover one and take one's breath away,
completely, a final time.

4.
The trains pass more frequently. The whistle
is blown less as if to avoid notice.
Sometimes I hear the train in the forest
and I stop shoveling. Do they watch
as I watch them?—a digger of graves

surrounded by shrubs, wood-sorrel, weeds.
Is their murmuring I can't hear prayer?
I cannot imagine their journey
or what they might say to one another
if anything, how the pain in their legs
must grow. Beneath the faces in the slats
a child might hold its mother's legs.
I hear only the sound of the train
and Ernst's coughing and the thud of earth
tossed up in piles beside the new grave.
Once in France, before the war, I rode
all day on a crowded train to Paris.
And at one stop a gang of boys
boarded, cussed loudly and drank wine.
As we departed, one boy calmly spat
on his window making the others laugh.
Beside me, an old woman shook her head
and said in all her years she had not seen
anything so awful. It seems odd now
that it mattered to her and not me,
and that I would choose to remember it
on this particular day, this moment.

5.
She thought it was unusual
when the prisoner started walking toward her
down the hill below the graveyard.
And for a moment she thought he was escaping,
but his stride was casual, slow.
His blond hair was cut short like a boy's.
She smiled at him as he tripped
crossing the ditchbank.
The water grew heavy in her pails,
but she did not think of lowering them.
One guard walked along the embankment
then sat down in the unmown grass.
As she spoke her name
she heard the other prisoners talking
as they worked—their words

seemed almost recognizable until she listened.
She had spent so much time learning not to listen,
not to hear the few gunshots at night,
or her mother in the next room
with the pocked-faced corporal from the motor pool
who swore he'd kill them both if they told anyone.
Her mother liked it.
Or else she wouldn't make those noises,
make herself sound like a pig.
Once she went out at night after stealing
the corporal's watch and buried it in a tin
among the rocks and red mud of the creekbed.
The crystal was chipped and the inscription,
in a language she did not know, was worn.
Sometimes she would wake and watch
the patrol walking outside her window
and hear the soldiers laugh loudly.
Sometimes she watched their faces lit
by the flare of a single match,
the way, now, the sun gave exact angles
to the prisoner's features.
He said very little. Hello. Asked her name.
He held out a clump of morning glories
he had found at the wood's shaded edge.
She lifted the pails slightly at her sides
to show she could not accept the gift.

6.
The man beside her cried.
But his cries were not
distinguishable from the others',
or from her own breathing,
or from the train.
She could not know
that by the second day
the man beside her would die
or that the infant
in the young woman's arms
had been dead all along,

but the woman would not let go,
that whatever prayers she said
would only consume
the boxcar's thin air.
The stronger passengers
pressed toward the slats.
She watched as lines of light
revealed the faces in the car.
She could not know
that later in the week
when she breathed the gas,
it would burn her throat
and when the woman around her
collapsed on the shower floor,
she would remain standing
for one moment, as if balancing,
the way she would balance
on the fallen logs as she walked home,
the two pails as counterweights,
and when she did fall
she would feel the floor
cold against her shoulders.
She could not know
that when her train passed
the prisoner looked up,
blocking the sun from his eyes,
but did not catch any one face in the slats.
He rested on his shovel
and began to dig again.
She could at times catch glimpses
of trees and the men
working along the roadside.
She could not know
that when her clothes were taken
to be deloused
she would be ashamed of her body,
its whiteness startling
in the cool light of afternoon,
and she would cover her new breasts
and the dark patch of hair

with her hands and arms
and realize she would never touch
herself as intimately
or with such a pure and generous fear.

7.
I often think of going back.
Curiosity. To see what's left there,
to see how the years have let the earth grow wild,
how the ferns and thistle have replaced
the small garden of flowers we planted.

Ernst was shot. Did I mention that before?
Desertion or looting. I can't remember.
Maybe he was trying to find his wife.
No. He wouldn't have died for her sake—
Maybe I was never told the right story.

I try not to think about it much,
but sometimes I think of being buried alive.
Everyone must have those thoughts, though.
I think one night a runaway Jew hid
in an empty grave I had dug.

In the morning I found nutshells, some crumbs
of bread, the impression of a body
on the soaked black earth. I hope
he survived, if he ever existed ....

ERIC PANKEY was born in Kansas City in 1959 and attended school in Raytown, Missouri. At the University of Missouri, he received a bachelor's degree in English and Education. In 1983, he completed his Master of Fine Arts in poetry at the University of Iowa. While a member of the Iowa Writers' Workshop he was awarded a Teaching/Writing Fellowship. He has taught creative writing at the primary, secondary and college level.